JE

$15

Do You Really Want a Horse?

Bridget Heos • Illustrated by Katya Longhi

amicus
illustrated

Amicus Illustrated is published by Amicus
P.O. Box 1329, Mankato, MN 56002
www.amicuspublishing.us

Library of Congress Cataloging-in-Publication Data
Heos, Bridget.
 Do you really want a horse? / by Bridget Heos ; illustrated by Katya Longhi.
    pages cm. — (Do you really want a pet?)
 Includes bibliographical references.
 Summary: "A horse (and the narrator) teach a young girl the responsibility—
and the joys—of owning a horse. Includes 'Is this pet right for me?' quiz"—
Provided by publisher.
 ISBN 978-1-60753-207-1 (library binding) — ISBN 978-1-60753-399-3 (ebook)
 1. Horses—Juvenile literature. I. Longhi, Katya, illustrator. II. Title.
 SF302.H467 2014
 636.1—dc23
                                    2012035933
Acknowledgements: Author Bridget Heos thanks horse owners Margy Whitaker,
Deb McLeod, Cathie McLeod, and Corey Dugan for their help with this book.
Wishing you many happy trails with Okoboji, Happy, Silhouette, and Tornadito!

Editor: Rebecca Glaser
Designer: The Design Lab

Printed in the United States of America at Corporate Graphics
in North Mankato, Minnesota.

Date 5-2014 PO 1224

10 9 8 7 6 5 4 3

About the Author

Bridget Heos is the author of more than
40 books for children and teens, including
What to Expect When You're Expecting Larvae
(2011, Lerner). She lives in Kansas City with
husband Justin, sons Johnny, Richie, and
J.J., plus a dog, cat, and Guinea pig.
You can visit her online at
www.authorbridgetheos.com.

About the Illustrator

Katya Longhi was born in southern Italy.
She studied illustration at the Nemo NT
Academy of Digital Arts in Florence. She loves
to create dream worlds with horses, flying
dogs, and princesses in her illustrations.
She currently lives in northern Italy
with her Prince Charming.

So you say you want a horse. You really, really want a horse.

But do you *really* want a horse?

If you have a horse, you'll need a pasture.

If you don't
have one…

Your horse is eating my flower garden.

. . . your horse will graze around the neighborhood.

The horse will need a field of grass and weeds about as big as a soccer field. To her, the pasture is one big buffet. She'll also need water and shelter. That can be a barn or shed.

Finally, she'll need...

. . . a friend: **You!**
Do you like trotting
on trails?

Leaping over fences?

Racing around barrels?

Your horse will…with you on her back!

You can ride together for fun and exercise…
or for sport. If you compete in rodeo or riding events,
your horse will be more than a pet…

. . . she'll be a teammate. Be a good teammate. Practice together as much as you can. While riding, be gentle but clear. She will listen.

Be positive! She'll like pats on the back, kind words, and treats. Just like you do after a job well done!

If you don't do this...

... she'll be offended. Really, you couldn't do it alone. Luckily, your horse has your back!

I'd like to see her jump those fences without me!

12

All that running and jumping makes your horse hungry. She'll need extra nutrition: oats and corn.

You'll need to do other things to keep
your horse healthy, too.
Clean her hooves.
Clip her nails.
Groom her.

See a vet regularly. Make sure she gets shots. She won't like all of these.

But if you don't take care of her...

. . . she could get sick.

I'm a little hoarse.

Even when she's healthy, be careful around your horse. Don't sneak up on her. Approach your horse from the side, not the front or behind. Talk to her as you come near.

If something spooks her, reassure her.
Remember, you're a team!

In cold weather, keep an eye on your horse. When the ground freezes, provide bales of hay in the field. In winter, she'll grow a heavy coat of fur! But on very cold days, a blanket is nice.

In the hot summer, make sure she has shade. Cool her with a wet sponge. Provide lots of water. Horses are a lot of work.

But you know who will always be happy to see you and give you a ride anywhere you want to go? Your horse!

So if you're willing to feed,
water, groom, provide shelter and
pasture, and spend time with your horse,
then maybe you really do want a horse.

Now I have a question for the horse.
You say you want a person.
You really, really want a person.

But do you *really* want a person?

QUIZ

Is this the right pet for me?

All pets need love and care. But horses require more time, work, and money than most pets. Is a horse right for you? Complete this quiz to get an idea. (Be sure to talk to breeders or horse rescuers, too!)

1. Will you be able to visit with and ride your horse often?
2. Can your family help you take care of a horse?
3. Do you have an acre of land on which to raise your horse?

If you answered . . .

a. NO TO ONE OR TWO, try riding lessons or horse camp to spend time with a horse instead of getting your own horse.

b. YES TO ONE AND TWO BUT NO TO THREE, consider boarding your horse at another stable or *leasing* a horse. *Leasing* means you help pay for some of the horse's food and boarding costs in exchange for getting to ride it and spend time with it.

c. YES TO ALL OF THE ABOVE, then you could care for your horse at home.

Websites

4-H Horse Curriculum
http://www.4-h.org/resource-library/curriculum/4-h-horse/
4-H is a national youth development organization. Their horse curriculum is available on their website, with many articles about horse care, safety, health, and riding.

National Little Britches Rodeo Association
http://www.nlbra.com/
The National Little Britches Rodeo Association is a group for rodeo riders ages 5-18. Its website has descriptions of events, competition schedules, and much more.

Responsible Horse Ownership:
The Humane Society of the United States
http://www.humanesociety.org/animals/horses/facts/responsible_horse_ownership.html
The Humane Society has articles and tips about what it takes to buy or adopt a horse, feeding, and general horse care.

US Pony Clubs
http://www.ponyclub.org/
The United States Pony Clubs, Inc., is a national youth organization that teaches horse care and riding techniques, and sponsors English riding and mounted sports events.

Read More

De la Bédoyère, Camilla. *Horses and Ponies*. Irvine, Calif.: QEB Publishing, 2010.

Niven, Felicia Lowenstein. *Learning to Care for a Horse*. Berkeley Heights, N.J.: Bailey Books/Enslow, 2011.

Owen, Ruth. *Horses*. New York: Windmill Books, 2012.

Ransford, Sandy. *Pony Care*. Irvine, Calif.: QEB Publishing, 2012.

Trueit, Trudi Strain. *Horse Care*. Tarrytown, NY: Marshall Cavendish, 2013.

Neigh!